1 and 2 Peter, Jude

Called for a Purpose

STEVE & DEE BRESTIN

FISHERMAN
BIBLE STUDY SERIES

1 & 2 PETER, JUDE

PUBLISHED BY WATERBROOK PRESS

12265 Oracle Boulevard, Suite 200

Colorado Springs, CO 80921

ISBN 978-0-87788-703-4

Published in the United States by WaterBrook Multnomah, an imprint of the Crown Publishing Group, a division of Random House Inc., New York.

Printed in the United States of America

2012

23 22 21 20 19 18 17 16

Contents

How to Use This Studyguide

*F*isherman studyguides are based on the inductive approach to Bible study. Inductive study is discovery study; we discover what the Bible says as we ask questions about its content and search for answers. This is quite different from the process in which a teacher *tells* a group *about* the Bible—what it means and what to do about it. In inductive study, God speaks directly to each of us through his Word.

A group functions best when a leader keeps the discussion on target, but the leader is neither the teacher nor the "answer person." A leader's responsibility is to *ask*—not *tell*. The answers come from the text itself as group members examine, discuss, and think together about the passage.

There are four kinds of questions in each study. The first is an *approach question.* Asked and answered before the Bible passage is read, this question breaks the ice and helps you start thinking about the topic of the Bible study. It begins to reveal where thoughts and feelings need to be transformed by Scripture.

Some of the earlier questions in each study are *observation questions*—who, what, where, when, and how—designed to help you learn some basic facts about the passage of Scripture.

Once you know what the Bible says, you need to ask, *What does it mean?* These *interpretation questions* help you discover the writer's basic message.

Next come *application questions,* which ask, *What does it mean to me?* They challenge you to live out the Scripture's life-transforming message.

Fisherman studyguides provide spaces between questions for jotting down responses as well as any related questions you would like to raise in the group. Each group member should have a copy of the studyguide and may take a turn in leading the group.

A group should use any accurate, modern translation of the Bible such as the *New International Version,* the *New American Standard Bible,* the *New Living Translation,* the *New Revised Standard Version,* the *New Jerusalem Bible,* or the *Good News Bible.* (Other translations or paraphrases of the Bible may be referred to when additional help is needed.) Bible commentaries should not be brought to a Bible study because they tend to dampen discussion and keep people from thinking for themselves.

Suggestions for Group Leaders

1. Thoroughly read and study the Bible passage before the meeting. Get a firm grasp on its themes and begin applying its teachings for yourself. Pray that the Holy Spirit will "guide you into all truth" (John 16:13) so that your leadership will guide others.

2. If any of the studyguide's questions seem ambiguous or unnatural to you, rephrase them, feeling free to add others that seem necessary to bring out the meaning of a verse.

3. Begin (and end) the study promptly. Start by asking someone to pray that every participant will both understand the passage and be open to its transforming power. Remember, the Holy Spirit is the teacher, not you!

4. Ask for volunteers to read the passages aloud.

5. As you ask the studyguide's questions in sequence, encourage everyone to participate in the discussion. If some are silent, try gently suggesting, "Let's have an answer from someone who hasn't spoken up yet."

6. If a question comes up that you can't answer, don't be afraid to admit that you're baffled. Assign the topic as a research project for someone to report on next week, or say, "I'll do some studying and let you know what I find out."

7. Keep the discussion moving, but be sure it stays focused. Though a certain number of tangents are inevitable, you'll want to quickly bring the discussion back to the topic at hand. Also, learn to pace the discussion so that you finish the lesson in the time allotted.

8. Don't be afraid of silences; some questions take time to answer, and some people need time to gather courage to speak. If silence persists, rephrase your question, but resist the temptation to answer it yourself.

9. If someone comes up with an answer that is clearly illogical or unbiblical, ask for further clarification: "What verse suggests that to you?"

10. Discourage overuse of cross references. Learn all you can from the passage at hand, while selectively incorporating a few important references suggested in the studyguide.

11. Some questions are marked with a ✐. This indicates that further information is available in the Leader's Notes at the back of the guide.

12. For more information on getting a new Bible study group started and keeping it functioning effectively, read *You Can Start a Bible Study Group* by Gladys M. Hunt and *Pilgrims in Progress: Growing Through Groups* by Jim and Carol Plueddemann. (Both books are available from WaterBrook Press.)

Suggestions for Group Members

1. Learn and apply the following ground rules for effective Bible study. (If new members join the group later, review these guidelines with the whole group.)

2. Remember that your goal is to learn all you can *from the Bible passage being studied.* Let it speak for itself without using Bible commentaries or other Bible passages. There is more than enough in each assigned passage to keep your group productively occupied for one session. Sticking to the passage saves the group from insecurity ("I don't have the right reference books—or the time to read anything else.") and confusion ("Where did *that* come from? I thought we were studying _____.").

3. Avoid the temptation to bring up those fascinating tangents that don't really grow out of the passage you are discussing. If the topic is of common interest, you can bring it up later in informal conversation after the study. Meanwhile, help one another stick to the subject.

4. Encourage one another to participate. People remember best what they discover and verbalize for

themselves. Some people are naturally shy, while others may be afraid of making a mistake. If your discussion is free and friendly and you show real interest in what other group members think and feel, the quieter ones will be more likely to speak up. Remember, the more people involved in a discussion, the richer it will be.

5. Guard yourself from answering too many questions or talking too much. Give others a chance to share their ideas. If you are one who participates easily, discipline yourself by counting to ten before you open your mouth.

6. Make personal, honest applications and commit yourself to letting God's Word change you.

Introduction

Why was I born? And what is the meaning of life, anyway? Can my longings ever be fulfilled, or am I caught in a trap of hopelessness?

If you've ever asked these questions, you've come to the right place. The letters of Peter and Jude were written to first-century Christians who were suffering great persecution under the cruel emperor Nero. They were tempted to give in to despair because of the crushing trials they faced. Peter wrote words of comfort and hope, reminding believers of their great calling and purpose.

Because of the living hope and special purpose Christ gives, Peter and Jude also challenged believers to remain faithful, to stand firm against false teaching, and to live holy lives.

CALLED FOR A PURPOSE

MATTHEW 4:17-20; JOHN 21:1-19; ACTS 4:8-13

hy am I living? What is the meaning of life? These were the thoughts I (Dee) had one rainy afternoon in 1965 as I sat mechanically smoothing, folding, and stacking diapers for the umpteenth time. I thought to myself: *Are my days going to consist of a never-ending chain of meaningless maintenance duties punctuated by a dinner out or a new sofa? I HATE THIS!*

I was spiritually blind when I asked those questions, unaware of the meaning God gives to life. After I gave my life to Christ, I learned that God has a holy purpose for our lives—a purpose that gives us living hope!

This purpose will become more clear as you study Peter's letters. In this study, we'll look at three passages that show how God called Peter.

1. What was it that first drew you to Jesus? What was your motivation for following him?

READ MATTHEW 4:17-20.

2. What message was Jesus proclaiming (verse 17)? What does it mean to *repent*? (Use a dictionary if you are unsure.)

3. For what purpose did Jesus call Peter (verse 19)? What does this mean?

4. For what purpose have you been called or chosen by God? If you can, write a general life purpose, based on Scripture, and then tell some specific ways you feel God wants you to fulfill that purpose.

After completing this guide, you may answer this question somewhat differently. Be open to what God's Word can teach you. You'll be asked to look back later and compare your answers.

5. When Peter followed Jesus, what did he leave behind (verse 20)? If you have responded to Jesus' call, what have you left behind?

READ JOHN 21:1-14.

These events occurred after Jesus' death and resurrection.

6. What do you learn about Peter from these verses? How could the Lord utilize Peter's character traits for his purpose of making Peter a seeker of people?

7. What distinctive character traits has God created in you? Think of a few specific ways that he might use these for his purposes.

READ JOHN 21:15-19.

8. Three times Jesus repeats another purpose he has for Peter's life. What is it? How is this purpose linked to Jesus' call to Peter to be a fisher of men?

6 1 & 2 PETER, JUDE

𝄪 9. What more does Jesus tell Peter in this passage?
What purpose will Peter's death serve?

READ ACTS 4:8-13.

10. What astonished the leaders about Peter and John
(verse 13)? Of what did they take note?

11. In what ways was Peter fulfilling God's purpose
for him?

𝄪 12. How well do you feel you are fulfilling the purpose
for which God chose you? In what areas do you see
growth? In what areas do you need the support of
this study group?

CALLED TO BE HOPEFUL

1 PETER 1:1-13

Alexander Pope wrote, "Hope springs eternal in the human breast." Thank God it does! When life's circumstances seem almost unbearable, it is hope that sustains us. *Hope,* as Peter uses it, means a "confident expectation," not a "hope-so" faith. Peter wrote to scattered believers who were suffering great persecution, reminding them of the living hope they had in Christ. He wanted them to remember this with confidence, so that, instead of crumbling, they would give glory to God. We too need to remember the great hope we have so that we will be prepared when suffering comes into our lives.

1. If you were introducing yourself through a letter, how would you describe yourself?

2. As an overview of the passage for this study, read
   1 Peter 1:1-12 on your own and find at least one
   reason, in each of the following verses, that should
   give a believer hope.

   verses 1-2

   verse 3

   verse 4

   verse 5

   verses 6-7

   verses 8-9

   verses 10-12

READ ALOUD 1 PETER 1:1-2.

✍ 3. To whom does Peter write? Where are they? Why does he call them "strangers"?

4. What opportunities do you have for contact with unbelievers? What could you do to increase these opportunities?

✍ 5. Can you remember a time when you were going through great suffering or stress but were able, because of your hope in God and his promises, to remain faithful? If so, share something about the hope you had at that time.

6. How does it make you feel to realize that you have been elected, or chosen, by God?

7. What aspects of salvation are seen in verse 2? What role does each member of the Trinity play?

8. Peter says we have been chosen for obedience to Jesus Christ. What are some specific ways you desire to be a more obedient Christian?

READ 1 PETER 1:3-13.

9. What do you learn about your inheritance in verses 3-5? What do you learn about God's power to sustain the believer? How does this make you feel?

10. What hope is there even in trials (verses 6-7)? Have you experienced this?

11. How was it possible for the recipients of Peter's letter to love Jesus, whom they had not seen (verse 8)? Why do you love Jesus?

12. How did the prophets gain their wisdom? How much did they understand of what they wrote? How is our understanding different from that of the prophets (verse 12)?

13. Because of our living hope, what does Peter exhort us to do in verse 13? Do you remember when you first had confidence in your salvation? Tell the group about it briefly.

14. Reflect on what you have learned from this study. What action might you take to better fulfill God's particular purpose for your life?

CALLED TO BE HOLY

1 PETER 1:13–2:3

uthor R. C. Sproul says, "We were created to shine forth to the world the holiness of God." But what does holiness look like? We are apt, as the Pharisees were, to reduce holiness to eating and drinking and other externals. We miss the deeper issues of righteousness. Charles Colson says that holy living must go beyond a self-focus "(those extra ten pounds, that annoying habit, maybe a quick temper).... *Holiness is obeying God*—loving one another as He loved us, finding ways to help those in need...." (Charles Colson, *Loving God*).

1. What are some synonyms for *holiness*? Describe a person you know who seems to have a holy lifestyle and character. How is he or she different from other people?

Read 1 Peter 1:13-16.

2. Why should we be holy (verses 15-16)? In what ways is God holy?

3. What instructions does Peter give in verses 13-14 for strengthening holy behavior? What are some practical ways to accomplish these instructions?

4. In what situations might you apply verse 13 to achieve holy behavior?

5. Put verse 14 in your own words. What pursuits have you abandoned as you have grown in the Lord? Why? What fills those time slots now?

READ 1 PETER 1:17-21.

6. What does verse 17 assume of the believer? What does God do according to this verse? How should you be living your life here on earth?

7. From what have you been redeemed (verse 18)? How was your life empty before you knew Christ? With what have you been redeemed (verse 19)?

8. Find at least six facts about Jesus in verses 19-21.

During your prayer time, spend some time worshiping Jesus by giving him praise for these truths.

READ 1 PETER 1:22–2:3.

9. What will be a result of holy living and obedience to the truth (1:22)?

Give an example from your life of the process of obedience leading to purity leading to love.

10. The Word of God gives us power for holy living. What do you learn about the Word in this passage (1:23-25)?

11. How are we to regard the Word? In what ways can the Word of God be spiritual milk?

How do you go about "drinking" spiritual milk from the Word? (Talk about specific personal examples.)

12. What relationship is there between holy living and habitual interaction with the Word? Explain.

13. Review the passage and this study. Pick one area of holy living to concentrate on this week, and ask the group to pray for you as you do this.

CALLED TO A NEW IDENTITY

1 PETER 2:4-12

*M*ost people struggle with feelings of low self-esteem. Peter's letters can help us to appreciate our incredible identity as chosen disciples of Christ. But it is also very important to realize that we have been chosen, not just to make us feel "special," but for a purpose! What grips us about Peter's letters is the way the apostle progressively reveals this purpose. Once our eyes have grown accustomed to the initial light of salvation, there is a whole rainbow of purposes that God longs to reveal to us. Do you know what God's will for you is during your time on earth? Peter has answers. And while we all have a need for healthy self-esteem, there is a dangerous tendency in the church today to elevate self rather than Christ.

This study shows that our purpose as chosen, holy people is to declare the praises of God!

1. What nicknames have you been called? How did you get these names?

READ 1 PETER 2:4-12.

2. What four things do we learn about Jesus Christ in verse 4? How is the life of a Christian similar to Christ's life in each of these ways?

3. What two word-pictures describe the believer in verse 5? What can you learn from each of these about your identity in Christ?

4. What is one duty of a priest according to verse 5? What does this mean?

5. What happens when believers don't understand they are all part of one building? What happens to local churches when the believers don't understand they are all priests?

6. What do you learn about those who trust in Jesus, the living Stone? What do you learn about those who do not believe (verses 5-8)?

7. What further description does Peter give of our identity in verse 9? (He repeats it in verse 10.) What does this mean to you?

8. What are some of the possessions, talents, or characteristics that God has given you which really belong to him? How are you or how could you be using these to "declare God's praises"?

9. In your own words and based on verses 4-12, describe your identity as a Christian.

10. Why is it important for believers to understand that they have been called to a new identity?

CALLED TO SUBMISSION IN THE WORLD

1 PETER 2:13-25; ACTS 4:5-7, 13-20

*J*n his book *Like Christ,* Andrew Murray writes: "Christian! Would you have strength to suffer wrong in the spirit in which Christ did? Accustom yourself in everything that happens, to recognize the hand and will of God.... Whether it be some great wrong that is done you, or some little offense that you meet in daily life, before you fix your thoughts on the person who did it, first be still, and remember, *God allows me to come into this trouble to see if I shall glorify Him in it....* With my eye turned from man to God, suffering wrong is not so hard as it seems."

1. When have you found it difficult to submit to someone in authority over you?

Read 1 Peter 2:13-17.

2. To whom are we told to submit in verses 13-14? Why? Give a few practical examples of this.

3. What effect does submission have on the talk of foolish people (verse 15)? Why does verse 15 follow verses 13-14? What might foolish people be saying concerning Christians?

4. How might you apply the above in addressing senators, school administrators, etc.—in writing or in person?

5. What guidelines to Christian freedom do these verses suggest?

6. What are some ways you can obey the commands in verse 17?

READ ACTS 4:5-7, 13-20.

7. Is there a conflict between Peter's behavior in this
    passage and his instructions in 1 Peter 2:13-17?
    Under what circumstances is it right for a Christian
    to disobey the government?

READ 1 PETER 2:18-25.

8. Compare the slave-master relationship to the
    employee-employer relationship. What guidelines
    do these verses give?

9. In the middle of this long passage on submission,
    Jesus, our role model, is held up to us. Find four
    things Jesus didn't do when treated unjustly. Find
    one thing he did do (verses 22-23).

10. 1 Peter 2:24-25 is the central message of the Bible—
    the Good News. Explain what each of the following
    phrases mean:

He himself bore our sins in his body on the tree,

so that we might die to sins

and live for righteousness;

by his wounds you have been healed.

For you were like sheep going astray…

11. What does this Good News mean for you personally in your various relationships?

12. Why do you think we are called to be submissive to the structures God has instituted (government, workplace, home)? How does Christ's example help you?

13. What do you want to remember from this study? What action could you take to better fulfill God's call to submission in your life?

CALLED TO SUBMISSION IN THE FAMILY

1 PETER 3:1-12

*I*t's one thing to live submissively to the authority figures God has ordained in the world at large. But now Peter becomes more personal, asking believers to mutually submit in the home and in the body of Christ. Sometimes this is a harder assignment!

1. Think about a marriage relationship you admire. What qualities make that marriage so attractive?

READ 1 PETER 3:1-7.

2. What situation is Peter describing in verse 1?

How is this similar to the situations in 1 Peter 2:18 and 23?

3. What hope does Peter offer to the woman who is submissive in this way?

4. What phrases does Peter use in verses 2 and 4 to describe a truly beautiful woman? If you are a woman, what could you do to make this description true of you?

5. How did Sarah show respect to Abraham (verses 5-6)? List some ways a Christian wife today could show respect to her husband.

6. Contrast putting your hope in God (verse 5) with giving way to fear (verse 6). Can you think of a situation in which you've had one of these responses?

7. Suppose your husband asks you to pray with him about a move or about increasing the size of your family. Discuss how you could respond, based on the two responses above (verses 5-6).

8. In verse 7, to whom does "in the same way" refer? (See 1 Peter 2:21 and 3:1.)

9. What warning does Peter give to the husband who fails to show his wife consideration and respect (verse 7)?

Read 1 Peter 3:8-12.

10. What difficult commands does Peter make in verses 9 and 11?

What encouraging promises are given in verses 9-10 and 12?

11. What do you want to remember from this study? What action could you take to "live in harmony with one another"?

CALLED TO COMPLETE DEVOTION TO CHRIST

1 PETER 3:13–4:2

*C*hristians receive a great deal of criticism—especially those willing to be on the "front lines." Sometimes we receive it face to face, as in a family or work situation. Often we receive it indirectly, through the mass media. Some of it is fair; much of it is not. Peter tells us how we should respond to this criticism.

1. Have you ever lost your temper or become sarcastically argumentative when criticized by an unbeliever? What effect did this have? Have you ever responded with genuine love to criticism? What effect did this have?

Read 1 Peter 3:13-17.

2. What question does Peter ask in verse 13? How does he qualify this in verse 14?

3. Give some examples of fears that might keep us from sharing our faith or working to implement change in our society.

4. The passage Peter is quoting in verse 14 is from Isaiah:

> Do not fear what they fear; do not be frightened.
> The LORD Almighty is the one you are to
> regard as holy, he is the one you are to fear, he
> is the one you are to dread, and he will be a
> sanctuary....(Isaiah 8:12-14)

If we fear God and nothing else, what promise does Isaiah give us?

5. What defensive measure does Peter suggest (verse 15)? What does this mean?

6. Verse 15 says, "Always be prepared to give an answer to everyone who asks you to give the reason for the hope that you have." Practice doing this by preparing a short testimony in the space below. Tell how the Good News became personal for you and how Christ makes a difference in your life. As time allows, share your testimony with the group.

7. What advice does Peter give in verse 16? What examples have you seen of this—in your life or in another's life?

8. What summary statement does Peter make in verse 17? Give an example from your own life of each of these two kinds of suffering.

READ I PETER 3:18–4:2.

9. This is a difficult passage. Read it slowly and find three examples of how a "death" or "dying to self" is followed by "life" or "being raised to a new hope" (3:18, 20-21).

10. Describe the mindset we need to adopt when suffering (4:1-2).

11. How would a Christlike attitude during suffering help a believer to abandon evil desires and live for the will of God (4:2)?

Ask the Lord to give you an opportunity to share your hope in Jesus with another person this next week—and then be alert, daily, for God's answer. You may give your testimony or simply ask if you could take a few minutes to discuss the central message of the Bible as part of an assignment for a class you are in. Be prepared to share the results with the group the next time you meet.

CALLED TO LIVE FOR GOD

1 PETER 4

*A*s a medical doctor, I (Steve) have noticed that some people grow through suffering while others fall apart. Should we as Christians expect to encounter suffering? If so, what should be our response? The trials that we experience may be different from the persecutions of Peter's day, but our response should be the same one Peter encouraged—a response based on a living hope in Christ.

1. As you think about your present stage of life, what do you think God's priorities are for you now?

READ 1 PETER 4:1-6.

2. Describe the purpose (verse 2) and the actions (verse 3) of the old way of life.

3. What activities should you leave behind because they have taken "enough time" from your life (verse 3)?

4. How might peers react when a new Christian breaks from a pagan lifestyle (verse 4)? Have you experienced this?

5. What sobering fact faces those who abuse the Christian (verse 5)?

Read 1 Peter 4:7-11.

6. According to verse 2, a Christian lives for the will of God. What specific aspects of God's will do you find in verses 7-9? Put the commands in your own words and then explain how you could specifically apply them to your life.

7. What is the purpose of a spiritual gift (verse 10)?

8. What does verse 11 add to your understanding of spiritual gifts? What examples have you seen of the two particular gifts Peter mentions?

READ 1 PETER 4:12-19.

9. Some say that a Christian should anticipate a trouble-free life of health, wealth, and success. What do these verses seem to indicate?

10. What should be the Christian response to suffering according to verses 12-14, 16, 19?

11. Based on this fourth chapter of 1 Peter, review the actions and attitudes that are central to God's purpose for you. How could you better align your life according to this calling?

CALLED TO ETERNAL GLORY

1 PETER 5

*T*he end of Peter's letter returns to his original reason for writing—to help young Christians stand firm in the time of testing. Peter calls for humility, alertness, and perseverance. Is there a reward? Yes!—eternal glory with Christ and a crown of glory that will never fade away.

1. What are some of your leadership responsibilities? Which are the most satisfying? The most frustrating?

READ 1 PETER 5:1-4.

2. On what authority does Peter appeal to church leaders (verse 1)?

&3. What positive characteristics of a shepherd or overseer does Peter stress in verses 2-3? What happens when the negative characteristics emerge in leadership?

4. Describe some of the pleasant jobs of shepherding. The less pleasant? How are they intertwined? (Think of the role of a teacher or parent as well as that of a pastor.)

READ 1 PETER 5:5-7.

5. Whom does Peter exhort to submission and humility in verses 5-6?

What are the rewards of humility?

&6. Briefly tell of one time when you consciously cast all your anxiety on God. How did he care for you?

READ 1 PETER 5:8-9.

7. How does Peter describe our enemy? How do you react to this description?

8. Two of Satan's common snares are pride and anxiety. Based on 1 Peter 5:5-7, how can you respond the next time Satan strikes?

9. What further advice does Peter give for dealing with our enemy (verses 8-9)?

READ 1 PETER 5:10-14.

10. These final comments can give us a key to the purpose of the whole letter. What themes stand out in this closing passage?

11. What has impressed you most in this closing chapter? What application will you make to your life?

CALLED TO RELY
ON GOD'S PROVISION

2 PETER 1

*D*oes the high standard of godliness in Peter's letters seem impossible to you? This study will encourage you! Today's passage points out clearly that God has made provision for salvation and for everything we need for a life that pleases God.

But there is also a challenge "to make your calling and election sure" (1:10). Michael Green says, "The New Testament characteristically makes room for both election and free will without attempting to resolve the apparent antinomy" (*2 Peter and Jude, Tyndale New Testament Commentaries*, pp. 73-74). And so must we. It is vital not only to understand God's part in the work of salvation but also to understand our part. This is what Peter emphasizes as he realizes his own death is near.

1. If God gave you a clear warning that you were going to die very soon, what truths would you be most anxious to impress on the hearts of those under your personal influence?

READ 2 PETER 1:1-4.

2. According to verse 1, how is faith obtained?

3. List all that God has provided for us to help us in
    the ongoing process of salvation and godliness
    (verses 1-4). What is our part in taking advantage
    of these provisions (verses 2-3)?

4. What two things will God's promises enable us to
    do? How can we get to know his promises better?
    What specific guidelines have you found helpful
    for daily interaction with God's Word?

READ 2 PETER 1:5-11.

5. Peter says, "For this very reason" we should practice
    the Christlike nature. To what reason is he referring
    (2 Peter 1:4)? How does he echo this in verse 8?

Peter emphasizes that while salvation is of God, our assurance of salvation grows as we see obedience and a Christlike nature reflected in our lives.

6. List the virtues that Peter says we should concentrate on in building our faith. What is the promise and the warning of verses 8-9?

7. Why is it so important to Peter that his readers make their calling and election sure (verse 10)?

READ 2 PETER 1:12-21.

8. What principles of discipleship does Peter model in verses 12-15? How are you following these principles with those under your spiritual care? Has someone done this for you?

9. What are some things that Peter says the Bible is *not* (verses 16, 20-21)? That it is (verses 19, 21)?

10. What do you learn about how the Bible came to us (verses 20-21)?

11. What has God impressed on you through this opening chapter of 2 Peter? What will you do about it?

CALLED TO COMBAT
FALSE TEACHING

2 PETER 2

*T*he warning about false teachers who seduce people away from the lordship of Christ is as relevant today as it was in Peter's day. As you study this passage, don't limit your thinking to the cults. Charles Colson writes: "I have spoken of the frontal assaults and the sneak attacks. There is something worse.... The enemy is in our midst. He has so infiltrated our camp that many simply no longer can tell an enemy from a friend, truth from heresy" (*The Struggle for Men's Hearts and Minds*).

1. What examples of false teaching *within* the church have you seen?

SCAN 2 PETER 2 ON YOUR OWN.

2. As an overview, what characteristics do you find of false teachers in each of the following verses:

Where will they be found (verse 1)?

Who do they deny (verse 1)?

What is their motive (verse 3)?

In what areas do they teach (verse 12)?

To what do they appeal (verse 18)?

What is the irony of their promise (verse 19)?

READ 2 PETER 2:1-3.

3. According to verse 1, what is the chief heresy of false teachers?

4. What is the consequence of false teaching (verse 2)? What examples of this have you seen?

READ 2 PETER 2:4-10.

5. This passage is one long statement. What parts make up the introduction (if…)? What part makes up the conclusion (then…)?

6. Although we do not see the righteous side of Lot's character in the Old Testament, Peter gives us some insight into his heart. What do you learn?

7. How do you respond to the condition of society today? How can you keep yourself from becoming desensitized to the evil in our society?

Read 2 Peter 2:11-18.

8. How is sin described in verses 10-18? How then can we avoid sin?

9. Give an example of a time when you felt the need to flee false teaching.

10. Who is particularly susceptible to false teaching (verses 14, 18)?

READ 2 PETER 2:19-22.

11. Give some examples of life pursuits that promise freedom but end in bondage.

12. How is backsliding described (verses 20-21)? How can we avoid this?

13. What specific warnings do you see for your life in this chapter?

STUDY 12

CALLED TO PREPARE FOR THE LORD'S RETURN

2 PETER 3

Billy Graham has said that if God does not judge our Western society, he will have to apologize to Sodom and Gomorrah!

Though the sin in our land is great, many scoff at the warning of a fiery judgment. People laugh at the idea of divine intervention. They consider the return of the Lord incredible. Yet Peter reminds us that God has intervened and brought judgment in the past, and that he has promised he will again. We who are believers need to live in recognition of this truth—living lives of holiness, diligence, and anticipation of that great and fearful day.

1. How would a person who equates his or her future with extinction think and live differently from a person who equates his or her future with the Second Coming of Christ?

Read 2 Peter 3:1-9.

2. Why does Peter say he is writing this letter (verses 1-2)? Why is it important to be continually reminded of God's truths?

3. How does lack of belief affect the scoffers' lifestyle (verse 3)? Can you give a contemporary example of how skepticism affects lifestyle?

4. What question do the skeptics ask (verse 4)? What similar questions are being asked today?

5. What faulty logic do the skeptics use to come to the conclusion that the Lord is not coming back (verse 4)?

Jude 8, 11, 19 and 2 Peter 2:10

Jude 10 and 2 Peter 2:12

Jude 12 and 2 Peter 2:13, 17

Jude 17-19 and 2 Peter 3:3

5. Can you think of examples of teachings that exhibit some of the warning signs given by Peter and Jude? List teachings and corresponding warning signs.

6. Jesus said that false prophets would come in sheep's clothing but "by their fruit you will recognize them" (Matthew 7:16). In this passage, Jude says they will be "without fruit" (verse 12). What fruit (or lack of fruit) should put you on guard about a leader, teacher, or elder in your midst?

READ JUDE 20-25.

7. What advice does Jude give to believers surrounded by false teachers (verses 20-21)?

8. Considering the people in your circle of influence, how might you specifically apply the commands in verses 22-23?

9. The doxology in verses 24-25 is well known and loved. How does its context within this letter add to your understanding of it?

10. In the opening study, you were asked to describe the purpose for which you had been called. Review the letters of Peter and Jude, paying particular attention to the opening and closing of each letter. Now think again about God's purpose or purposes for your life. Describe these and tell some specific ways you feel led to fulfill these purposes. (Compare with your answer to study 1, question 4.) How has your perspective changed or broadened?

Leader's Notes

Study 1: Called for a Purpose

Question 9. "Ancient writers state that, about thirty-four years after this, Peter was crucified; and that he deemed it so glorious a thing to die for Christ that he begged to be crucified with his head downwards, not considering himself worthy to die in the same posture in which his Lord did" (Adam Clarke, *Clarke's Commentary: Matthew–Revelation,* p. 663. Nashville: Abingdon, 1832).

Question 12. If time permits, hear from everyone, giving individuals the option to "pass."

Study 2: Called to Be Hopeful

Question 3. In the Greek, "strangers" means those who have settled down alongside pagans in the world. In other words, we have been chosen to mix with the world—to be in the world, but not of it.

Question 5. Encourage group members to be brief so that all can share.

Question 9. In 1 Peter 1:3-5, salvation is seen in all its tenses. "Christians *have been* born anew by the mercy of God, *are being* guarded by the power of God, and *look forward* to obtaining complete deliverance from all evil in the last time" (David

Wheaton, *The New Bible Commentary, Revised,* p. 1239. Grand Rapids, Mich.: Eerdmans, 1970).

Question 10. Gold, when held over the fire, loses it impurities. Only what is genuine remains. To facilitate sharing, you could ask people to share how specific trials rearranged their priorities, strengthened their faith, or urged them to love more wholeheartedly.

STUDY 3: CALLED TO BE HOLY

Question 3. The newer translations of 1 Peter 1:13 say, "prepare your minds" (NIV) or "brace up your minds" (Phillips). The older translations say, "gird up the loins of your mind" (KJV). This phrase brings to mind the men of Peter's day pulling up their long robes and tying them out of the way so they could get to work. Today we might roll up our sleeves. Holy living takes concentration and planning!

Question 5. Remember to focus on adding positive behavior as well as eliminating the negative.

Question 9. One example from my (Dee's) life: When I obeyed the Lord's command to keep my tongue from evil (1 Peter 3:10), my life became purer, and love in my relationships increased.

STUDY 4: CALLED TO A NEW IDENTITY

Question 2. Three times in 1 Peter we read that Jesus was chosen by God. Seven times we read that believers are chosen, elected, or called by God. Just as we didn't merit salvation, but were simply chosen, neither do we merit the daily ways God chooses to watch over us. We do need, however, to increase our alertness to the hand of God in our lives—as well as the *purpose* for which he has chosen and watched over us.

STUDY 5: CALLED TO SUBMISSION IN THE WORLD

Question 3. "Peter's advice sounds like Jesus' in Matthew 5:16; If your actions are above reproach, even hostile people will end up praising God. Peter's readers were scattered among Gentiles who were inclined to believe vicious lies about Christians. Attractive, gracious, upright behavior on the part of Christians could show these rumors to be false and could even win some of the unsaved critics to the Lord's side" (*Life Application Bible,* p. 1932. Wheaton, Ill.: Tyndale House Publishers, 1988).

Question 8. "Many Christians were household servants. It would be easy for them to submit to masters who were gentle and kind, but Peter encouraged loyalty and persistence even in the face of unjust treatment" (*Life Application Bible,* p. 1932).

STUDY 6: CALLED TO SUBMISSION IN THE FAMILY

Question 2. The KJV comes close to the literal meaning when it translates 1 Peter 3:1 "…if any (husband) obey not the word." In other words, the husband may be a believer or an unbeliever who is living in disobedience, and the wife's obedience will help win him over to godliness.

Just as God calls believers to be submissive and respectful to government officials and employers who may be corrupt, so a woman should show submission and respect to a husband who may be corrupt. However, if he asks her to do something that is against God (such as submit to abuse or cooperate in sin), she should refuse. That may mean separation with the insistence that he get help. (A helpful resource is *Love Must Be Tough* by James Dobson.)

Question 8. Commentators vary on what "weaker" partner means. Phillips paraphrases this as "physically weaker yet equally heirs with you in the grace of life." Others say that because the woman has just been told to be submissive to her husband, the man is being cautioned against taking unfair advantage of her submissiveness.

Study 7: Called to Complete Devotion to Christ

Question 5. J. B. Phillips expresses the Greek well in his paraphrase of 1 Peter 3:14-15: "And if it should happen that you suffer 'for righteousness sake,' that is a privilege. You need neither fear their threats nor worry about them; simply concentrate on being completely devoted to Christ in your hearts."

Study 8: Called to Live for God

Question 9. First Peter was written shortly before Nero's persecution of the Christians in A.D. 64. The prospect for the Christians' future was far from trouble-free! Peter told them to expect suffering. Likewise, every believer experiences suffering, since God's ways are in opposition to the world's ways; culture will always run counter to the way Christians strive to live.

STUDY 9: CALLED TO ETERNAL GLORY

Question 3. Leadership can be dangerous! Often those who are in authority lose touch with the people they lead and they act arrogantly. Peter stresses that leadership is service, not domination.

Question 6. "Most translations, unfortunately, begin 1 Peter 5:7 as a new sentence (*Cast all your anxiety on him*). This breaks the close connection with what precedes. The Greek text continues by means of a participle the sentence that began with verse 6. When we turn ourselves over to God in every situation of life, knowing that the One who led his people out of Egyptian slavery has allowed our affliction and is in full control, we are enabled to cast our anxieties on him. To recognize his hand in life's trials is to be freed from the anxiety they produce" (Robert H. Mounce, *A Living Hope*, p. 87. Grand Rapids, Mich.: Eerdmans, 1982).

STUDY 10: CALLED TO RELY ON GOD'S PROVISION

Question 7. "Peter wants to rouse the complacent believers who have listened to the false teachers and believe that because salvation is not based on good works they can live as they want. If you truly belong to the Lord, he says, your hard work will prove it. If you're not working for God, maybe you don't belong to him. If you are the Lord's—and your hard work backs up you claim—you will never be led astray by false teaching or glamorous sin" (*Life Application Bible*, p. 1940).

Study 11: Called to Combat False Teaching

Question 7. When we stop being shocked by sin, we are in trouble. It is easy to become accepting of sin when it is so commonplace. But we should pray that God will keep us outraged by sin.

Question 9. Encourage group members to think of times when they recognized false teaching in a cult, in the mass media, or within the ranks of Christianity.

Keith Brooks has compiled a helpful brochure showing the scriptural error of the cults (*The Spirit of Truth and the Spirit of Error*, Chicago: Moody Press, 1969).

Study 12: Called to Prepare for the Lord's Return

Question 5. The scoffers tried to say that the Lord was *negligent* in carrying through on his promises. But Peter points out that Jesus' delay in coming back is because of God's *patience.* He wants people to be saved.

Study 13: Called to Persevere in Faith

Question 3. Jude had intended to write a letter about salvation, but news of heresy prompted him to write a short, strong letter exposing false teachers who rejected the lordship of Christ.

Question 4. In Jude 11, "Jude offers three examples of men who did whatever they wanted (verse 10)—Cain, who murdered his brother out of vengeful jealousy (Genesis 4:1-16);

Balaam, who prophesied to get money, not out of obedience to God's command (Numbers 22-24); and Korah, who rebelled against God's divinely appointed leaders, wanting the power for himself (Numbers 16:1-35). These stories illustrate attitudes that are typical of false teachers—pride, selfishness, jealousy, greed, lust for power, and disregard of God's will" (*Life Application Bible,* p. 1964).

The Fisherman Bible Studyguide Series—
Get Hooked on Studying God's Word

Old Testament Studies

Genesis

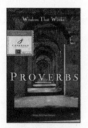

Proverbs

Acts 1-12

Acts 13-28

Colossians

James

New Testament Studies

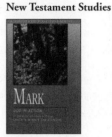

Mark

John

Romans

Philippians

1, 2, 3 John

Revelation

Women of the Word

*Becoming Women
of Purpose*

*Wisdom for
Today's Woman*

Women Like Us

*Women Who
Believed God*

Topical Studies

Building Your House on the Lord

Discipleship

Encouraging Others

The Fruit of the Spirit

Growing Through Life's Challenges

Guidance and God's Will

Higher Ground

Lifestyle Priorities

The Parables of Jesus

Parenting with Purpose and Grace

Prayer

Proverbs & Parables

The Sermon on the Mount

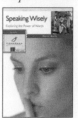

Speaking Wisely

Spiritual Disciplines

Spiritual Gifts

Spiritual Warfare

The Ten Commandments

When Faith Is All You Have

Who Is the Holy Spirit?